Global-Wide Souvenirs
N.Y. 2012

How do I get here?

What do I really want?

I just want to leave footprints
while I'm walking this life.

Publication created by Carlos R. Chavez
eMail : carlitosregidor@hotmail.com
Associated : Eduardo M. Suarez , Rosa E. Cespedes

© Carlos R. Chavez

Love Sculpture

© Carlos R. Chavez

© Carlos R. Chavez

Flatiron Building

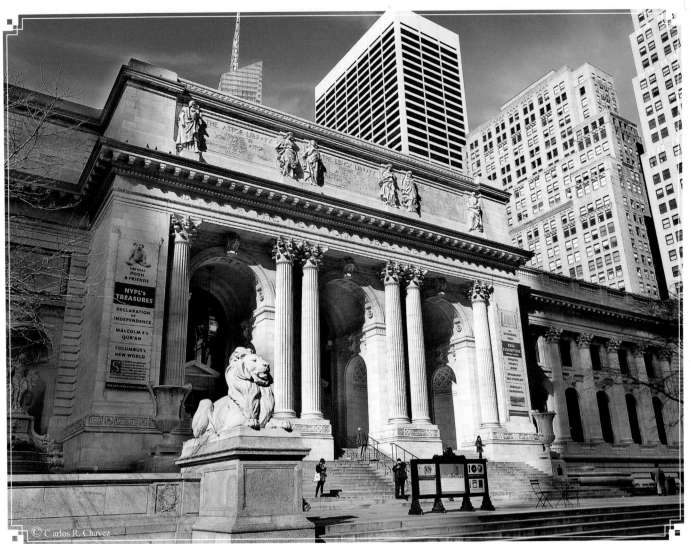

New York Public Library

Horse-Drawn Carriages

Jacqueline Kennedy Onassis Reservoir

8   Angel of the Waters (Bethesda Fountain)

Gapstow Bridge Central Park

9

© Carlos R. Chavez

© Carlos R. Chavez

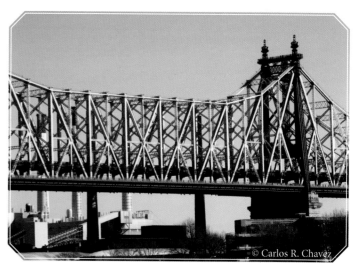

© Carlos R. Chavez

Queensboro Bridge

© Carlos R. Chavez

Queensboro Bridge vie from Manhattan

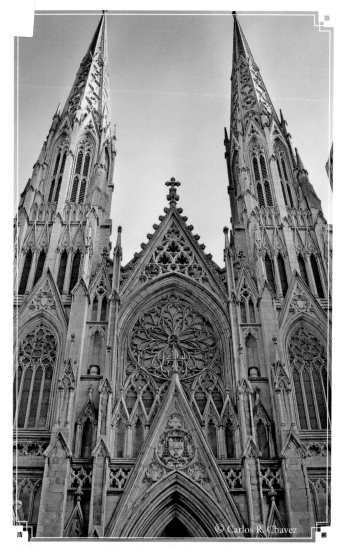

12   *Saint Patrick's Cathedral*   *John Paul II*

© Carlos R. Chavez

© Carlos R. C havez

Chrysler Building

Times Square

Criminal Courts of N.Y.

15

LET US RAISE A STANDARD TO WHICH THE WISE
AND THE HONEST CAN REPAIR THE EVENT
IS IN THE HAND OF GOD
WASHINGTON

© Carlos R. Chavez

Washington Square Arch

© Carlos R. Chavez

© Carlos R. Chavez

Christmas Tree Rockefeller Center

Atlas Rockefeller Center

Bowling Green Station

© Carlos R. Chavez

Four _ Faced Clock (Gran Central)

© Carlos R. Chavez

Gun outside UN Building N.Y.

© Carlos R. Chavez

Sphere Within a Sphere Sculpture at the U.N.

19

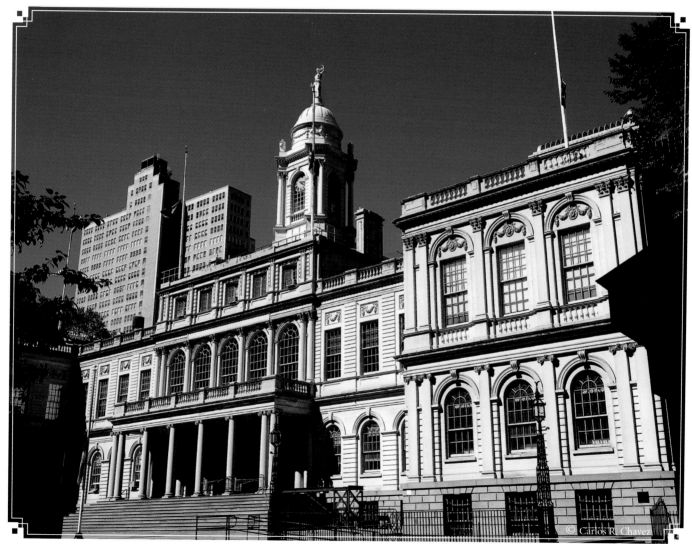

© Carlos R. Chavez

City Hall of N.Y.

Dumbo (Manhattan Bridge)

© Carlos R. Chavez

Wall Street

New York Stock Exchange

George Washington

© Carlos R. Chavez

Broocklyn Bridge

Ellis Island Immigration Museum

25

Dobble Check (Zucotty Park)

Romeo and Juliet   Central Park

© Carlos R. Chavez

Charging Bull   Bowling Green Park

© Carlos R. Chavez

© Carlos R. Chavez

The Eagle Battery Park

Governors Island Ferry Waiting Room

© Carlos R. Chavez

© Carlos R. Chavez

Times Square   *Woolworth Building*

An Italian Journey
Drawings from the Tobey Collection: Correggio to Tiepolo

VIENNA CIRCA 1780
An Imperial Sitter Service Rediscovered

AMERICAN WOMA
FASHIONING A NATIONAL IDEN

PICASS

Museum of Modern Art MoMA

Natural History Museum New York

Natural History Museum New York

© Carlos R. Chavez

The Sphere and Forest of Flags

© Carlos R. Chavez

Eternal Flame

© Carlos R. Chavez

The Sphere 10ᵗʰ Aniversary

Bowling Green Park

© Carlos R. Chavez

Bronx Zoo

© Carlos R. Chavez

New York Aquarium Coney Island 37

© Carlos R. Chavez

Freedom Tower and Memorial Park 9/18/2011

© Carlos R. Chavez

Cities Service Building

© Carlos R. Chavez

Woolworth Building

© Carlos R. Chavez

© Carlos R. Chavez

40   *Statue of Liberty*   *Woolworth Building west view*

© Carlos R. Chavez

Manhattan Bridge view from Manhattan

41

© Carlos R. Chavez

© Carlos R. Chavez

Empire State Building

Peking (ship) South Sea Port

© Carlos R. Chavez

© Carlos R. Chavez

San Remo Apartments view from Central Park

"Dumbo" Manhattan Bridge

© Carlos R. Chavez

Lincoln Center

West Broadway Building

Radiator Building

© Carlos R. Chavez

World Finantial Center view from Exchange Place

Broockyn Bridge

48 "Reflecting Absence"

Winter Garden

© Carlos R. Chavez

The Church Building

© Carlos R. Chavez

Nogushi's Red Cube

New World Trade Center design
view from Exchange Place NJ